What's inside?

D0291634

the dirt

5 get the dirt what are you really getting into?

to do it or not to do it?

8 calling all virgins beat the haven't-done-it blues

12 8 simple steps to sex how to get from flirt to hurt

14 quiz time are you ready for sex?

44 pressure cooker romance who's pushing who to have sex

95 ultimate sex formula the secret to great sex revealed at last

41, 112 top 10s of sex all the reasons you've been looking for

safe sex—fact or fiction?

17 reality tv goes hollywood reality tv like you've never seen it before

18 condom talk the performance review you can't afford to skip

23 surf's up find out what can't stop those pesky swimmers

26 2 is better than 1? or is it? the absolute truth about double bagging

28 when he gives you flowers what it really means

30 and baby makes 3? what to expect when the unexpected happens

32 got rhythm? gramps sets the record straight

34 early exit strategy how well does it work?

42 dateline chicago the scandalous inside story

48 zero tolerance abstinence's shocking side effects

CORRECTION:

It has come to our attention that teen drug and alcohol use is not the top reason for adolescent pregnancy—teen sex is.

What's *farther inside*?

52 **exclusive interview** a real teen dad tells all

54 **look out** for the gift that keeps on giving

76 **greek tragedy** one disease's plan of attack

79 **nothing to lose** too late to save yourself—now what?

82 **sowhattayaknow?** test yourself

92 **once upon a time** when a frog becomes a prince

96 **more than meets the eye** the risks no one's talking about

contrary to popular belief

36 **verdict's in** is oral sex really sex?

55 **born to be gay** what do genes have to do with it?

59 **but i don't like girls** when opposites don't attract

62 **gurl 2 gurl** does girl time mean gay time?

63 **dream analysis** your subconscious desires revealed!

66 **size up the situation** do you measure up?

83 **say what?** find out if what you've heard is true

89 **restroom wisdom** juicy tidbits you won't hear anywhere else

truth time

68 **man makeover** what it takes

107 **no going back** how to deal when you wish you hadn't

114 **got God?** created to connect, that's you

119 **the dirt is done**

CORRECTION:

Sex is not the most important thing to a teen as reported in the article entitled, "Sex Is the Most Important Thing to a Teen." Apparently, teens can still be extremely horny, curious, and have enough hormones flowing through their body to arouse a small pachyderm—but other issues are important to them. Education ranks high on the list of mega-important stuff. So do sports, God, friends, future, college, confidence, and happiness. None of which are enhanced by sex. We apologize to anyone who felt like a weirdo-loser for not thinking about sex 24/7. So get out of your Spiderman pj's and go get your mom to fix your lunch, 'cuz you can show your face at school today. It's okay, we called your teacher. But we told her about the pj's.

get the **Dirt**

Hey you! Yeah you, reading this book. Sit down, we need to talk. Listen, we have talked about lots of things together. We have looked at how to be *Dateable*. We have discussed why girls are crazy and why guys are jerks. We've hit some really big stuff. But there is something else that we need to talk about. I've been putting it off, but it's time, and I think you're ready. We need to have "the talk."

Yeah, I know it's embarrassing, and it's as uncomfortable for me as it is for you. But here we go.

It's like this: There are these bees and . . . and some birds. And see, the bees are . . . well, they like the birds. You know? More than *just friends*. I mean they *like* 'em like 'em. . . .Okay, that makes no sense. I don't know anything about birds and bees.

How 'bout this: It's like a flower. Yeah, you are a beautiful flower. And in the spring you will open up and blossom. And then a bee will come and do whatever bees do . . . ?

Ugh! Start over. Here's what I am trying to say. When a man and a woman love each other, well, they "love" each other, and sometimes this makes a seed grow in the woman, and that seed becomes a flower that opens in the spring, and a bee comes and makes a baby. . . . Aaaghhhh! I can't do this.

Scrap it! Here's the deal. **We're about to talk about s.e.x.** Ya know, sex. You've heard about it. You've thought about it. You see it plastered all over the media. But it seems like no one wants to talk about it. Oh, sure, they'll dance around it and convince themselves they are hitting the issues, but c'mon. Not many people just talk plain truth. Either they want to tell you that you're going to hell for doing it or they tell you to explore every little urge you have. Both of these leave you twisted, confused, and bitter. That's not who I am. Nope. We are about to look at this stuff full-on and give you the reals.

justin lookadoo

Justin Lookadoo
author-in-chief
(basically the one to blame if this book offends you)

Warning
to the Easily Offended

If you are one of those people who are easily offended and you prefer the softened, candy-coated answers that are cute and cuddly like a little lap dog, then **you need to put this book down now**. 'Cause when you turn the page, your little lap dog is going to turn into a crazed pit bull and come after you full force. Yeah, you will probably be offended. So you might want to get a milder, tamer book on the sex issues. This ain't it.

Also, if you are reading this book so you can find all the exceptions, go for it. Every rule has a bunch of exceptions, and this stuff is no different. So if you have nothing better to do with your life than to send me a lengthy e-mail listing all your exceptions, feel free. Do it. I will read it because I have nothing better to do with my free time, plus, I want to make fun of you.

For those of you still with me, **let's get our sex-truth on**. You may wanna stretch a little before you get going—we don't want anyone to get hurt. And definitely wait 30 minutes after eating before you jump in. So here we go.

It's real. It's raw. It's true. It's *The Dirt on Sex.*

Calling ■ All
Virgins

Will all virgins please stand! C'mon. We're waiting. What? Okay, we know that's not all of you. Not even close. Three of you stood up, and there are way more virgins than that. In fact, about half of you with your hands on this book should have stood up.

That's right. You may feel like the last remaining virgin on the face of the earth, but you're not. The real story is that the studies say that about half of all teens have had sex. But do you know what that means? About half have NOT! Holy schlumpa! How could that be? I know what you're thinking: If there are that many virgins running around, then why do I feel like the lone leper virgin? Well, I'm glad I pretended you asked.

Media Madness ● ● ● ● ● ● ● ● ● ● ● ●

First, and most obvious, check out the media. Now I am not one of those all-media-is-Satan kind of guys. Not at all. But in this case, it may be true. You know how hard it is to catch a DVD, CD, or mag without skin-flashin' and sex-talkin'. It's like that's all there is.

People say the media has no influence on teen sex. These are the same people who have been cracking down on how much smoking is going on in the media. Why? Because they admit that the media influences people's decision to smoke. Now wait. You

can't have it both ways. Either it has an influence or it doesn't.
And it does. ◉ ◉ ◉ ◉ ◉ ◉ ◉ ◉ ◉ ◉ ◉ ◉ ◉ ◉ ◉ ◉ ◉

Loudmouths

Another big issue is that of the loudmouths. They are the ones who have had sex and keep talking about it. If this is happening around you, you need to know that these people have some major issues they need to deal with.

We can agree that sex is a very personal thing, so if someone is spouting off about it to everyone, then they either:

1. feel guilty and are trying to convince themselves it was okay by convincing you that it is
2. are searching for an ego boost to make themselves feel like a man
3. don't understand the connection that sex brings

None of these are good reasons to be blabbin'. And what happens on a bigger level is all this talk makes it sound like more people are doing it. They're not. It's just that the one who has is talking the loudest.

Liars

Then you have the liars. You know these people. They are the ones who have never had sex but for some reason feel better about themselves if they make people believe they have. Twisted? Yes. They have serious self-issues that they need to deal with. 𝔻

Myth #1

• • •

Everyone

is doing it

except you.

VIGILANTE
Virgins

Okay, not everyone is doing it. So what are you supposed to do? Shout to the world at the top of your lungs, "Hello world, I'm a virgin!" Uh . . . no, don't do that. Some people out there are like that. They are what I call the "Vigilante Virgins." The ones who wear their virginity like a badge of courage. A trophy. It becomes their identity. They meet someone with a cordial greeting of, "My name is Cindy, and I'm a virgin. How 'bout you?"

Here's the problem with the VVs. If that becomes your identity, then when you do get married and have sex, you will have some major psycho-head issues because you have not lost just your virginity, you have lost your identity.

Here's my suggestion. Yeah, commit to saving sex until you are committed to a marriage. Keep yourself out of the danger zones. (Check out our book *Dateable* for more on this.) And then just accept this as the way it's supposed to be. Not a point of discussion, argument, or identity. Your virginity is not the real issue here. It's your life. Commit to your passion, to your success, to the excitement life has for you. Don't be ashamed to say you're a virgin when the sex topic comes up (and it will!). But don't try to beat everyone up with it. Be confident in who you are, and you will be what the VVs wish they were—cool, secure, and unshakeable. 🌀

8 Simple Steps to Sex

The Hug

The Hand-Hold

The Flirt

The Look

The sex process includes all of this stuff. Not just the intercourse. These 8 steps are varying degrees of walking into the pool of sexuality. They're just different levels of it. Fellas, if kissing is not part sexual, then go do it with the rest of the football team. (No, really, don't!)

Here's the prob. Sex has been so dissected and twisted that people define sex as merely intercourse. That is so wrong. By then, most of the sex is over. That is just kind of the exclamation point on sex.

Just look at the progression. With each step you have a greater level of risk. Each time you make a bigger physical investment in the relationship, the stakes get higher, and you have more to lose.

The Kiss | The Make-Out | The Touching/Fondling | The Intercourse

This progression isn't a bad thing. It's part of a natural development that takes you from the first glimpse of a crushable cutie to the ultimate love connection of marriage. So don't be afraid of it. Just control it. Don't just run through the steps with some guy in your class. And definitely don't bounce around the ladder.

Take the steps slowly. Think through the investment and the risk. Get into the higher steps only when you have the high-level commitment. And then you will be able to enjoy the process and not have to worry about the risks.

Are You Ready for Sex?

1
I *really* love the person. T F

2
I want to take our relationship to a deeper level. T F

3
I can handle the emotional issues of sex. T F

4
We have the birth control and STD issues handled. T F

5
We are married. T F

Scoring

1. T = 20, F = 0
2. T = 15, F = 0
3. T = 10, F = 0
4. T = 15, F = 0
5. T = 1000, F = 0

0–60: Hold the Hormones. None of this makes you ready to have sex. Yeah, people say that it is okay if you are ready. But listen, sex is a marriage game. It's not about how you feel, it's about where you are. Hey, you may *feel* ready to go fishing, but if you're not near some water, you're *not* ready.

Being ready for sex is all about pure love with giving and receiving. That kind of thing can only be given to someone that you have a total commitment with, not just an "I really like you" kind of thing.

I have advised a lot of teens about sex and relationships. I have not met one, *not one!,* who got into sex because of pure motives. I have heard all kinds of reasons:

bf/gf is pressuring me
friends are pressuring me
so my bf won't leave
to feel loved
to prove I'm not gay
we were bored
you have to do it some-time, why not now
we're in love

Not one of these reasons works. Listen to me carefully again. Being ready has nothing to do with how you feel. It is based on where you are in life! Bottom line: If you aren't married, you aren't ready.

1000–1060: Sex It Up! Yeah, it's a loaded quiz, but then again, it's a loaded question. If you scored this high, then party on. Make love. Have sex. Get freaky. Do it. Whatever you want to call it, just get it on. Especially if you hit the 1060 mark. You are definitely in the right place in life, you have the right motives, and you have covered the consequences and what ifs. So why are you sitting there reading this book? Go get some.

Myth #4

•••

Sex is okay

when you are

ready.

Reality TV goes Hollywood

This season a movie icon and a TV powerhouse will hit the reality rollercoaster and reveal what happens when the cameras aren't rolling.

James Bond has proven himself to be the super-funk of the spy world. Cool beyond cool. He is always saving the world and hooking up with a secret agent hottie in the name of national security. It's a beautiful woman, in a beautiful place, making beautiful love.

This season we take a closer look and connect reality to the big screen. According to the smart people who keep track of this kind of stuff (like the American Social Health Association), odds are that of all the women Bond romps with, every fourth one has an STD. It's reality TV at its best. We get to **follow 007 to the clinic**, where we see the horror on his face as the doctor tells him he has herpes. We continue to tag along on his journey of embarrassment to the pharmacy to get his prescription filled. Through the shame, depression, and anger, we go past reality TV and straight to real life.

———

Next in our special report, the reality is exposed on one of our favorite *Friends*, a show so full of life yet so void of reality. Sure, we have seen a pregnancy, but that has been turned into a beautiful experience with absolutely no negatives. But it's a must-see when our cameras reveal the shocking truth: If 1 of every 4 Americans has an STD, one of our friends has something they are way too embarrassed to share with the others—but apparently they are sharing it with other partners. You don't want to miss it.

Condom

Welcome to *Condom Talk,* where you get to discuss your questions about condoms and safe sex. You got the questions? We got the answers.

(*Condom Talk* was previously recorded live in front of a fictitious studio audience asking fictitious questions and receiving real answers.)

CT: Don't condoms prevent STDs and pregnancy?

It's true that this is the battle cry of the condom supporters. So let's simply define one little word:

pre·vent (pri-'vent): to keep from happening

So the prophylactic proponents want you to believe that condoms keep pregnancy and STDs from happening. But they do not prevent anything. They *help* prevent this stuff. The only way to prevent it is abstinence.

CT: How effective are condoms in helping prevent pregnancy?

Condoms have an 84 to 87% effectiveness rate in preventing pregnancy. That sounds good unless you're one of the 15% that ends up with a surprise stork visit.

Check it. Condoms average about 85% effectiveness when used very carefully, every time, exactly right, no flaws. So, basically, they are effective when they are used in a controlled, clinical environment. When was the last time you heard of someone having sex in a controlled, clinical environment? (If someone you know has, the doctor needs to be arrested, 'cause something ain't right.) That is not where people are getting it on. So for teens the failure rate is probably much higher than 15%.

CT: How effective are they against STDs?

That is a tougher question. Start with HIV.

The effectiveness rate for HIV is 80%. Did you catch that? Turn it around. 20% of the time condoms are not effective in stopping HIV. That means 20 out of every 100 people who were counting on condoms to protect them will die of AIDS.

CT: Wait a sec. HIV and pregnancy are both semen issues. So how can it be that the effectiveness is 85% for pregnancy and only 80% for HIV?

No one really knows. The best guess we can come up with has to do with behavior and frequency. Check it. The pregnancy statistics are for heterosexual couples only. (Duh, right?) The HIV infection rate is for everyone. So with that statistic there are a lot of people thrown into the number pool who can't get pregnant, so with condom failure they can catch HIV without getting pregnant. Plus, some sex acts are a lot riskier and increase the failure rate as well.

This agrees with the statement by the people at the Global Health Council. They said, "Condoms appear to be marginally less effective for reducing HIV infection than for preventing

If you want all the gory details on this stuff, look it up yourself. Here's where to get it: S. Weller and K. Davis, "Condom Effectiveness in Reducing Heterosexual HIV Transmission," Cochrane Methodology Report in *The Cochrane Library*, Issue 4, 2003 (Chichester, UK: John Wiley & Sons, Ltd). Also check out www.medinstitute.org.

pregnancy." The bad news is you die, but the good news is you weren't pregnant.

CT: Well, what about the rest of the STDs? Do condoms work on them?

For that answer we have to go to the big dogs. I mean, the National Institute of Allergy and Infectious Diseases, National Institutes of Health, and Department of Health and Human Services. The big dogs. Their report on the effectiveness of condoms in preventing STDs other than HIV concluded this:

> **"THERE IS INSUFFICIENT EVIDENCE TO PROVE CONDOM PROTECTION AGAINST STDs."**

This includes stuff like herpes, HPV (genital warts), syphilis, gonorrhea, chlamydia, cytomegalovirus, chancroid, and some other diseases we can't pronounce.

So basically they gave condoms a seal of approval of "Who knows?"

Boy, that's what you want to hear when your life depends on it, eh? "Hey, will this save my life?" "Who knows?" "Okay, I'll take it."

CT: **So what are you saying? If someone is going to have sex they shouldn't even use a condom 'cause they aren't really foolproof?**

No, that is not what we are saying. Condoms can *help*. But don't act all surprised if you get pregnant or an STD. It's a risk. So if you put yourself in that situation, it's better than nothing.

It's like this. If someone is going to shoot at you, yeah, put on a bulletproof vest. They may shoot you in the face, but hey, it's better than nothing.

Me? I would rather not be shot at. Duh. It's called abstinence. Problem solved.

Myth #54

• • •

If you douche right after sex, you won't get pregnant.

We let our surfer-intern-guy explain what happens when a girl douches after sex to try to keep from getting pregnant.

Okay, like, pretend like one of those little sperm guys is a surfer dude. So, like, what happens is, like, during sex, the guy's stuff comes out of him and goes into the chica girl. Well, that's like the surfer dude paddlin' on his board trying to pick up speed. What happens when the girl does the douche thing after the sex thing is she shoots this rush of water up in there. That's like a massive wave rollin' up on the sperm dude. And then what happens is the little spermazoids catch the wave and hang ten all the way to shore . . . uh . . . I mean, all the way to the egg. Then Mrs. Egg and Mr. Sperm have a little beach throw-down, but instead of roasting a pig, they cook up another little surfer dude. Right on.

(Note: This is best read with the voice in your head sounding like a surfer.)

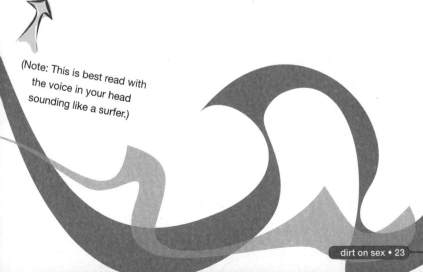

Myth #11

•••

If you pee right after sex, you won't get pregnant.

We let the surfer intern answer one last question. Will urinating right after having sex keep a girl from getting pregnant?

Dude, I don't know how me taking a leak would, like, have any effect on a girl . . . oh, you mean if the *girl* pees. Yeah, I knew that. And the answer is B, no way, my reader-type people. A girl's pee tube and her baby tube don't criss-cross. They got their own things going. So you can pee all day long, and those little guys are going to keep on swimmin'. C-ya.

2 Is Better than 1?

Scientific Factoid:

Using two condoms (double bagging) *increases* the risk of STDs and pregnancy.

How can this be, you ask?
Let me explain by getting all scientifical.

Friction: The resistance to motion that is called into play when attempting to slide one surface over another with which it is in contact. The frictional force opposing the motion is equal to the moving force up to a value known as the limiting friction. Any increase in the moving force will then cause slipping. Static friction is the value of the limiting friction just before slipping occurs. Kinetic friction is the value of the limiting friction after slipping has occurred. This is slightly less than the static friction. The coefficient of friction is the ratio of the limiting friction to the normal reaction between the sliding surfaces. It is constant for a given pair of surfaces. The energy lost due to friction is usually converted to heat.

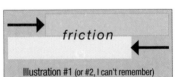

friction

Illustration #1 (or #2, I can't remember)
2 objects sliding over one another and causing friction. To get the full effect, look at this illustration while sitting in a sauna set to about 98.6°.

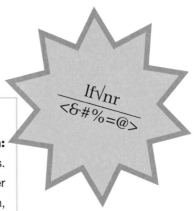

$$\frac{lf\sqrt{nr}}{<\&\#\%=@>}$$

Mumbo-Jumbo Breakdown:
Here's what all that crap means. You put two pieces of rubber together and start moving them, and the result is friction. Friction breaks stuff down and creates heat, which aids in breaking things down even quicker. Then take into consideration that if these two condoms were used in sex, the rubber would be surrounded by bodies at approximately 98.6° F. This heat would further aid in the breakdown. So the basic scientific finding is that you are stupid if you put two rubbers together and expect better protection, because they will both break down and become ineffective.

HA! Six years of biology finally paid off.

And you said I would never use it . . . well, take **THAT**, *Daaad!*

Cherokee Rose *(rosa laevigata)* – white with yellow stamen and large single blooms. This is a spring flower that has a moderate fragrance. They grow best with 6 hours of sun per day, and morning sun is preferred. Irrigate twice per week.

Lady Tulip *(tulipa clusiana)* – rosy red petals that are white inside. Plant them at 60° or below in September or early October. They grow best in full sun and well-prepared soil with fast drainage.

FLOWERS

Chlamydia
(chlamydia trachomatis) – symptoms show up 7–21 days after sex. They may be minimal or not at all. Between 50 and 75% of people who have it have no symptoms. Girls: Symptoms include discharge and bleeding between periods, burning or pain while urinating, abdomen pain, and sometimes fever and nausea. Guys: Watery white discharge and burning or pain while urinating.

When allowed to grow and flourish, chlamydia can lead to more serious infections and even organ damage. Chlamydia is the most commonly reported infectious disease in the U.S. and is also classified as one of the most dangerous infections among women today.

It can be cured with proper diagnosis and medication.

And Baby Makes 3?

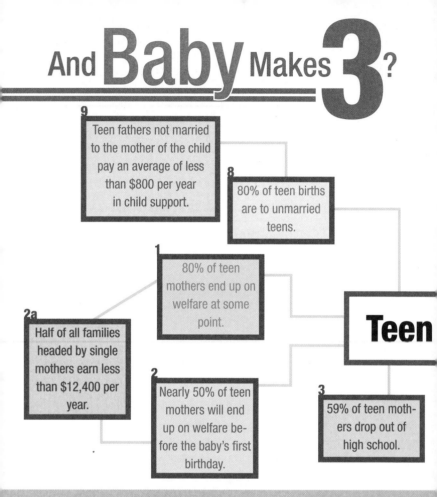

9 Teen fathers not married to the mother of the child pay an average of less than $800 per year in child support.

8 80% of teen births are to unmarried teens.

1 80% of teen mothers end up on welfare at some point.

2a Half of all families headed by single mothers earn less than $12,400 per year.

2 Nearly 50% of teen mothers will end up on welfare before the baby's first birthday.

Teen

3 59% of teen mothers drop out of high school.

Obvious Conclusion Stated for the Slow People: If you are a teen and you get pregnant, you are on your own. The "sperm donor" will not be there to help. Most teen moms will drop out of school and be on welfare at some point.

Hope: If you are a teen mom, it doesn't have to be this way for you. There is hope. You can find ways to succeed and even flourish. It will be hard. It will be the battle of

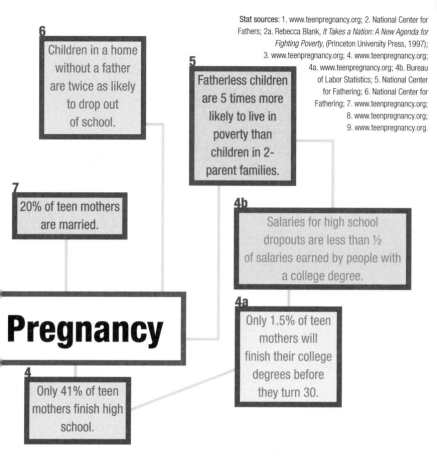

Stat sources: 1. www.teenpregnancy.org; 2. National Center for Fathers; 2a. Rebecca Blank, *It Takes a Nation: A New Agenda for Fighting Poverty*, (Princeton University Press, 1997); 3. www.teenpregnancy.org; 4. www.teenpregnancy.org; 4a. www.teenpregnancy.org; 4b. Bureau of Labor Statistics; 5. National Center for Fathering; 6. National Center for Fathering; 7. www.teenpregnancy.org; 8. www.teenpregnancy.org; 9. www.teenpregnancy.org.

6
Children in a home without a father are twice as likely to drop out of school.

5
Fatherless children are 5 times more likely to live in poverty than children in 2-parent families.

7
20% of teen mothers are married.

4b
Salaries for high school dropouts are less than ½ of salaries earned by people with a college degree.

Pregnancy

4a
Only 1.5% of teen mothers will finish their college degrees before they turn 30.

4
Only 41% of teen mothers finish high school.

your life. No, it will be the battle *for* your life. You can win. But that's a different book for a different time. Start, though, by talking with the parentals, counselors, youth pastors, everyone you can to get your game plan together. Remember, it is not what happens to you that is important but how you react to what happens to you.

Go Ask Grandpa!

Grandpa, I heard that if you have sex with a girl during her period or just a few days after, she can't get pregnant. Is that true?

Ah, the rhythm method. That's what they call it, my boy, when people have sex only at certain times of the month so she won't get pregnant. It's called the rhythm method, but I call it a gamble.

Hey, I've got a joke for you: What do you call people who use the rhythm method for birth control? *Parents!* Heh, heh, heh . . . [cough] . . . [cough] . . . excuse me. . . . Now what were we talking about? Oh yeah, sex at certain times of the month to prevent pregnancy.

You look confused, boy. Let me explain. You know how I told you a woman's mind and emotions are unpredictable? Well, that's nothing compared to how her body can be. When a girl has her period, it's nature's way of cleaning her body and getting rid of the egg that was in her. And she usually doesn't have another egg available for about 14 days. Notice I said "about." Remember that word. Then this ovalteen . . . uh . . . opalnation . . . no, *ovulation,* that's it—this ovulation thing happens, and then another egg is available. Well, the theory is that you can have sex during this no-egg time and she won't get pregnant. The problem is that none of this is exact science. There may be an egg available day one, or there may not be one at all that month. You just don't know. Add this to the fact that a sperm may stay alive and on the prowl looking for an egg inside her body for up to four or five days, and you start getting some major risks.

So remember, if you decide to have sex and use the rhythm, you could be singing the blues! . . . Heh heh . . . [cough] . . . Now move away from the TV, it's time for *Wheel of Fortune.*

Early Exit Strategy

DID YOU KNOW?

If a guy pulls out before he finishes (ejaculates), the girl can still get pregnant.

A watery-gooey liquid is released from the penis before a guy ejaculates.

A guy does not feel the release of this fluid.

The first few drops of semen have the highest concentration of sperm.

Many times a guy doesn't know when he is going to climax until it's too late.

Myth #12

• • •

Sex
is the most
important
thing in a
teen's life.

We interrupt your reading to bring
you this late-breaking news . . .

ORAL SEX IS SEX!

Researchers discovered this by asking each other these
extremely scientific questions:

How are each of these classified?

	Sex	Not Sex
Sex	✓	
Good Sex	✓	
Bad Sex	✓	
Fast Sex	✓	
Slow Sex	✓	
Anal Sex	✓	
Oral Sex	✓	

In a **unanimous decision**, our researchers concluded
that all of these activities are in fact sex. They also concluded
that many people *believe* that oral sex is *not* sex. They also
found that many people *believed* wrestling was real. But
just the fact that they believed it did not classify them as
"right." It classified them as "idiots."

Excuse me for a sec, I need to have a
word with the editor. Hey, Editor Person, this next part is getting R-rated, and
you'll want to cut it, but leave this stuff
in 'cause it's way important. Okay?

Many people also feel that oral sex is no big deal. If that is your belief, please answer the following questions.

(Note: If you believe that oral sex is sex and is a big deal, then you may want to skip past these disturbing questions.)

1. Describe in detail the body part you are giving oral sex to. What does it look like? What does it feel like, smell like, etc.?

2. Does it have any birthmarks, zits, or other markings?

3. Does it have any open sores, bumps, or other skin irregularities?

4. Where is the last place this body part was before you placed your mouth there?

5. When was the last time this body part was cleaned? When was it last checked by a doctor?

6. Have you asked the person attached to this body part any of these questions?

7. How will you respond when your 15-year-old daughter tells you she is going to a party and she is going to place the penises of John, Charles, Raymond, and Alex in her mouth?

If you said, "*Eww*," "Yuck," "Gross," "*No way*," or "That's embarrassing," then here is your question: If you are too yucked out and embarrassed to examine the body part, talk about it, or ask the person about it, does it make sense that you would put your face there?

Our group of unscientific scientists has also discovered that girls get into oral sex for the same reasons that they get into traditional sex. They are looking for acceptance, status and popularity, connection, love, admiration, or adventure. Ladies, you need to understand this. It's going to be harsh but true. If you think oral sex is not sex and not a big deal and so start giving it to a guy, then all you have become to him is a hole. This is not love; it is not respect or even affection. It's exploitation.

> **If you start giving oral sex to a guy, all you are to him is a hole.**

We're not surprised that the increase of teens having oral sex has also brought an increase in teen depression. Even our dim-witted scientist posers could figure this one out.

Rejection is a major side effect of oral sex. This is one of the most intimate and emotionally risky things that two people can do, but it is treated like a sneeze that you "excuse." There is no way you can feel secure about yourself in this sitch. With oral sex you give the power to destroy you to the other person—a person you aren't even committed to. Yeah, you may be committed to dating each other. That is not a commitment; that is a hobby. So the investment is total exposure and vulnerability, and the payoff is total rejection because you are now nothing special. Just a place to get off.

Then comes the guilt—the rush of self-hate because you have given someone a very private, intimate experience and it

Guys will tell it! If you are having oral sex with a dude, more than likely he's gonna tell it. Everything you did. Everything you touched or kissed. Why shouldn't he? If you believe it's no big deal to do, then it's no big deal to tell.

was treated as a joke or a topic of discussion with friends, the topic right after the debate over pepperoni versus supreme. Yes, some people will tell you that you will get over the guilt and everything will be cool. Guess what? You're not supposed to get past the guilt! It is there for a specific purpose. And that purpose is to get you to stop. Just like the burning sensation is your cue to take your hand off the stove and go get ice, the guilt feeling is your cue to stop what you are doing and run to the Creator to let him clean you up again.

The problem of oral sex and guilt begins to build on itself like a hurricane in warm waters. The depression causes a person to look for an escape. Oral sex offers an escape, which brings rejection, guilt, and depression, which again looks for an escape . . . and the cycle continues, on and on until the person is emotionally, spiritually, and physically destroyed. This cycle leads to low self-worth. You feel like you are a loser because you have given out for free what God had declared is valuable and costs a lifetime commitment of marriage.

If oral sex is no biggie, then you should be able to show pics to your teacher, parents, youth pastor, and grandma.

The theoretical question that must be addressed now is: "How do I get and/or stay free from the oral sex trap?"

Our research entitled "How to Not Be Stupid: A Practical Guide to Oral Sex . . . Uh, and How to NOT Do It" has provided useful insight. Here are some steps:

1. **Get out of the sitch.** You know times when o.s. is going to be happening or expected to happen. A party, movie night, back of the bus, a date. Evaluate the situation in advance, and then . . . no show. Skip the scene and go do your own thing.

2. **Buddy up.** There's strength in numbers. Find some buds who believe the same as you, and stick together. It's going to be a battle, but you are war-worthy. You've got what it takes. Make a pact with your squad that no matter what one person wants to do, the group has the right to get obnoxious and interfere. This is going to be way important 'cause at some point one of you will break down and give in. That's the time for action. The squad has to swoop in, break it up, and bounce out.

3. **Operation Secret Freedom.** It's time to go underground and take back your friends. Slowly start bringing up the fact that you and your buds are getting out of the oral scene and staying out. You're going to find out that a lot more people feel just like you. Slowly, one by one, bring them to freedom. You will have to go viral and infiltrate on the DL, because if you just bust up on some party, announce your revolt, and call for people

> **Girls, don't wait till some dude is dropping his pants to decide to make a plan.**

to follow you, you will get totally Talibanned, and no one will be helped. Bust through the front door, and you're a mega-decibel weirdo. Sneak in the back, and you are the silent warrior of freedom.

A word from our researchers: It may sound like we are anti-oral. That is so not the case. I mean, how would we talk? How would we eat? But listen, we know that o.s. is a risk. Like any other kind of sex, it's a marriage game. So in a loving marriage where you have the respect, the commitment, and the total acceptance of each other, hey, go for it.

Top 10 Bad Reasons to Have Sex

10. Ya gotta do it sometime
9. My bf wants to
8. My friends are making fun of me
7. I'm horny
6. To feel loved
5. It feels good
4. Boredom
3. We're ready
2. We're going to get married anyway
1. We love each other

Dateline Chicago

Al "Scarface" Capone, notorious gangster and Public Enemy Number One, has died today. In a surprising turn of events, it was not a mob hit or an assassination that took his life—it was syphilis.

Capone began his life of crime in the sixth grade. His reputation as a gangster quickly grew, and he was promoted to Chicago. He rose to power and eventually took over the Chicago crime organization.

Even though many murders took place during his reign as mob boss, Capone always had an alibi that placed him far away from the crime scene. The most notorious murder that took place at his direction was the St. Valentine's Day Massacre, which took the lives of seven rival gangsters.

While living the life of crime, he also lived the life of luxury and desire. He was a true ladies' man—so much so that no one really knows which girl gave him syphilis. Since the symptoms take 3 to 4 weeks to show up, it was anyone's guess. And even if Capone saw the symptoms of the first stage, he probably didn't know what he had, because the first symptom is a painless, reddish-brown sore on the nose or mouth. Even untreated, it will go away in 4 to 6 weeks. Then the second stage symptoms would have shown up 6 weeks to 6 months later. Again, misdiagnosis was possible as it shows up as a rash anywhere on the body, many times on the palms of the hands, soles of the feet, and genital area. All of this can be accompanied by flu-like symptoms that can further confuse diagnosis. All of these symptoms may go away, but the infection doesn't. Left untreated, it can cause heart disease, brain damage, blindness, and even death.

Scarface was convicted of tax evasion and sent to the toughest prison in the world.

Upon arriving at Alcatraz, he was diagnosed with syphilitic dementia, brain damage due to syphilis.

After serving almost 7 years in prison, Capone was released. But because of the deterioration of his mind due to the undiagnosed and untreated syphilis, the most notorious gangster, Al "Scarface" Capone, died in seclusion from a curable infection.

Editor's Note: Syphilis is curable with antibiotics. But since most people don't have severe symptoms or don't recognize the ones they have, the infection usually goes undiagnosed and is left to cause irreversible damage.

Pressure Cooker

Romance

Cooker

[kissing . . . soft sighs]

Guy: . . . Oh, baby, you feel sooo good.

Girl: You do too.

Guy: I have never had anyone make me feel the way you make me feel.

Girl: Really?

Guy: Yeah, I just want to get so close to you, soul to soul, skin on skin . . .

Girls, you might have been there. You might have felt the pressure to get physical that can come from a guy. He's got all these hormones running through his bod. He will tell you all kinds of things. How much you mean to him. How he knows that you were meant to be together. (You know this. But if you need a refresher, go get the book *Dateable*. It's all in there.)

But the **soul-crushing pressure** can really come from yourself. You are looking for that emotion. That rush of feeling loved, accepted. You want to make the guy happy so he will like you more and more. This is your own internal pressure that you need to understand and handle. You need to trust God and his Word and know that you are good, lovely, and beautiful without anyone else.

But pogo back with me to the fellas. A lot of guys, especially the ones who haven't gotten straight with Christ, are going to put the squeeze on you. Don't trust them just 'cuz they seem like a "nice guy." Without Christ at the center, you just can't trust anyone to have your best interests at heart. They will tell you that it's because they care so much about you. But listen, this is their own pressure talking—pressure that comes from a totally different place. Guys who listen to the rules of the world might hear something like this from their "pals":

Guy 1: So, have you done her yet?

Guy 2: Naw, man.

Guy 1: What, you can't get it up?

Guy 2: That's not what our relationship is all about.

Guy 1: Yeah, I understand. You're gay.

Guy 2: Shut up.

Guy 1: Oh, go cry to your mama, you big wuss.

Guy 2: Man, just get off it.

Guy 1: Hey, you don't mind if I ask your girl out, do ya?

Guy 2: What?!

Guy 1: I just thought she'd like to see what it was like to be with a real man.

Guys can live in a high-pressure world. They will hound each other, make fun of each other, bash each other about anything. Especially when it comes to sex. It doesn't matter if the other guys have done it or not. Everyone will make fun of him. They will be trashing him about what he is *not* doing and lying about what they *are* doing. And even the "nice guy" forgets all concept of truth and honor when he is getting made fun of. So he will pick up the challenge and take it to the girl.

Guy 1: So? Have you done her yet?

Guy 2: Yeah.

Guy 1: When?

Guy 2: Friday after the game.

Guy 1: Was she good?

Guy 2: Yeah, she was alright.

Guy 1: Tell it.

Guy 2: After the game we all went over to Brent's house to go swimming. Well, I took her in the house, and we went in the game room. And I just went for it.

Girls, connect the dots here. If you have sex with your bf because he pressured you, then more than likely the crazy-pressure came from his friends. So you were used to make him look good with his friends. Ah, true love.

Note from the Author: Before you cop a ghetti-tude and say that there are exceptions and that this is not the way it always happens, let me give you a suggestion: Don't bother! I am hitting the norms. The way it usually happens. Guys get pressured by their friends, and girls get pressured by the guys. Not all guys are like this—some are totally sold out on Christ—but be honest with yourself, is the guy you like really sold out, or are you lying to yourself? Whew! I'm glad we had this conversation. Now move on. I'm tired and want to take a nap.

Abstinence
Has Been Found
to Have **Serious**
Side Effects

The stupidest quote ever is brought to you by the Centers for Disease Control and Prevention. In their Morbidity and Mortality Weekly Report they find that:

Abstinence has a pregnancy prevention failure rate of 26%.

So what they are saying is that abstinence is even less effective than condoms in preventing pregnancy. Am I the idiot here? 'Cause I don't get it. How can abstinence fail in preventing pregnancy? Apparently I don't know the definition of abstinence. Hold on, I'll go look it up. Okay, here it is:

Abstinence is the trait of abstaining.

Well, thanks, Sherlock. Don't you love poo definitions like that? Alright, let's go down to the root word, *abstain.*

Here, *abstain* is *to not do something.* So, like I thought, abstaining from sex means not doing it. So for that 26% failure to happen, *somebody* was having sex! 'Cause if you are abstaining, you are not doing it. When you have sex, guess what? You are no longer abstaining, you are sexing. **Abstinence has a 100% success rate** . . . duh!

But check it, there are some other major side effects of abstinence.

Great Sex

That's right—abstinence gets you primed for sex. If you stay sex-free until you are married, you will get the ultimate sex pay-off. Go check out "The ULTIMATE Sex Formula Revealed."

Confident Catch

Remaining abstinent will help boost your confidence. First, you will not be opening yourself up to the ultimate rejection that sex brings. When you expose your body to someone like that, your entire self-esteem is in their hands. You become oversensitive to every comment made. But when you stay out of the sex zone, you don't worry about it. You are in control of your life, and your self-worth is not in the hands of someone who has seen you naked.

Second, you have what others wish they still had. When you remain sexually pure, you become, well, untouchable. And you will be seen as valuable. I mean, what is more valuable, a beat-up car that everyone trashes or a new car in mint condition? It's a no-brainer. It's the same with people. Which girl is seen as more valuable? This girl no one has ever touched, or the one everyone has touched?

Realizing all of this will let you see yourself as valuable. You will be able to look people in the eyes. You'll be less stressed. It will be like you are living in this alternate reality where the things that are messing with other people's lives don't affect you at all, and you'll totally give off that confident vibe.

Creator Connection

God totally wants you to connect with him. He made sex to create major spiritual and emotional attachments. So if you stay away from the sex scene outside of marriage, then you will be able to focus on him better. You won't be torn between your connection with a person and your connection with God. You won't have any guilt, feel any shame, or be faking that you are living for God while you're really doing your own thing. A way-cool verse in Psalms says, "If the LORD delights in a man's way, he makes his steps firm; though he stumble, he will not fall, for the LORD upholds him with his hand" (chapter 37, verses 23–24). That's you. That's now. Save yourself for the best sex ever in the marriage God will give you.

Yep, there are major side effects to abstinence. And they're all good. You will be the one who is prized, valued, and soul-connected to the Creator. So stay sex-free and get you some killer side effects.

Myth #97

• • •

If I get
pregnant
my boyfriend
will be there
with me.

Teen TELLS ALL Dad

jlook: So how old is your little girl?

Darren: Four months yesterday.

jlook: Wow. When was the last time you saw her?

Darren: Two weeks ago.

jlook: So are you and the mama still together?

Darren: Naw, man, I have a girlfriend. Besides, I'm going away to college in a couple of months, and I don't want to be attached.

jlook: So you're not going to be attached to your daughter?

Darren: Yeah, I'll see her whenever I come back to town.

jlook: Well, how'd you end up with a kid? I mean, I know how, but, well, you know what I mean.

Darren: Yeah, I know what you mean. We were bored.

jlook: Don't you have TV?

Darren: It's like this. She is 15, and her parents wouldn't let her go out on dates, so we just hung out at her house all the time. Well, there was nothing else to do, so we started having sex at her house. So, yeah, basically, we were just bored.

jlook: You starting sexing 'cause you were bored.

Darren: Yeah.

jlook: Are you bored now?

Darren: Yeah, kind of.

jlook: Uh . . . I gotta go.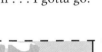

Chef Pepe's recipe for "A Bun in the Oven"

1 bored female

1 bored male

– Let simmer together with lots of free time

– Add raging hormones

– Let bake for nine months, and it's ready to deliver!

Gonorrhea
The Gift That Keeps on Giving

> This page has been brought to you by gonorrhea,
> the gift that keeps on giving.

Order now

and symptoms will arrive in 2–21 days after having sex.

Or maybe they won't, because many people
never see any symptoms at all. But if you do . . .

Girls, expect a lovely thick greenish-yellowish discharge
and abnormal vaginal bleeding. Plus, you get to receive
burning or pain when going #1 or #2.

Guys, you also get to have the yellow-green yuck ooz-
ing from your penis. And, you guessed it, the same pee-
pain.

And as an added bonus:

If not treated, gonorrhea can cause some serious infections, damaged reproductive organs, and the great
possibility that a mother will pass it to her baby.

If you are not fully satisfied with gonorrhea, you can go to the doctor for antibiotics.
But the legal department says we must warn you that, like the flu, many strains of
gonorrhea are becoming more resistant to antibiotics. So don't wait.

Act now!

I'm Gay,

and God Made Me That Way!

People being gay has so much more to it than guys dressing nice and talking with a lisp and girls getting short haircuts and playing contact sports. I know what you're thinking, "If that doesn't make you gay, then what does?" Well, the gay scientists—you know, the people who study homosexuality—they argue over how being gay happens. And they have boiled it down to two options:

1 You are gay because of your environment.

2 You are born gay.

Being gay because of your environment can mean lots of things. You could have been abused physically or emotionally. Maybe one or both of your parents were total butt-heads. Or maybe they weren't even around. Maybe you got trapped in porn addiction. I don't know. So many things could be involved here.

When I talk with people in schools and conferences and they say, "I'm gay," I simply ask, "What's the payoff of being gay?" They always look at me weird, but I explain there has to be

some kind of payoff. For some reason for them, being straight equals pain. It's not just because "that's the way you are." Nope. There is pain associated with heterosexuality and a payoff associated with homosexuality. So what is it?

In asking people questions, **I have not found one person who had pure motives for being gay.** They have all been running from something else. A girl I spoke with at the end of the school year said she was gay. When we got down to it, her dad was verbally and sometimes physically abusive. Her uncle was the same way. They always called her stupid and ugly. They made fun of her teeth and her clothes. Everything about her. Even her last two boyfriends did the exact same thing. (See a pattern here? She didn't . . .) Oh yeah, and her parents hate gay people.

So she switched to girls. Not because she's gay but because she is running from the major negatives that guys have put into her life. Plus, she's trying to get back at her parents. Now she is really freaking out because she's got all these life and family problems plus this gay issue she is bringing on herself.

Then there is the "I was born gay" argument. Well, poop on that.

Check it. Can we agree that God makes people different? Basic. Simple. Some are tall, some short. Some are energetic, some mellow. Some artistic and others mechanical. We are different.

Some kids are over-the-top hyperactive and aggressive. Right? You've seen 'em. They are the ones running through stores just trashing the place. Tearing stuff down, running, yelling, just going crazy. They are the ones who see a ball on the ground and run as fast as they can to pounce on it.

Question: This little kid was born aggressive, so does that make him a criminal sitting in jail for road-raging and shooting someone who pulled in front of him on the highway?

Genetics has pre-wired him with aggressive tendencies. But that does not make him a criminal. Same thing with this genetic gay tendency. Genetics has pre-wired some guys with what we consider feminine tendencies. They may be sensitive. They may like to play with dolls. They may be able to buy clothes that match without anyone's help. But none of this makes them gay. It just makes them different. Just like everyone else is different.

Then the obvious Q: "What *does* make someone gay?" Answer: Their choices. That's it. It's not what happens to you. It's not your wiring. It's your choice. You choose what you do. You control what thoughts you focus on in your mind. You choose whether or not you are going to be gay by what you let bounce around and grow in your mind.

Some studies claim some guys have an extra Y chromosome in their DNA soup that could make them more aggressive. In fact, they believe that a lot of people in prison have this extra Y. But a lot of people are also running free with this genetic makeup. Does that make them criminals too? No. The criminals' choices made them criminals.

Before you get all hyper on me, catch the hint. I am not saying gay people are criminals, and I'm not comparing being gay to being a convict. The argument is about genetics. Let's blow a major hole in the argument of the genetics-makes-you-gay theory. This is simple stuff. For the gay gene to survive and multiply, as some gay activists claim, then gay people would have to be mating. Okay, what's wrong with this picture? Steve and Bob are not going to reproduce. Just simple genetics shows that the gay gene pool should be getting smaller, not larger. The argument people want to throw out to that is "Well, gay is a recessive gene like being blonde, but there are lots of blonde people running around. Their pool hasn't gotten smaller." Simple answer. Blonde people can reproduce!

Bottom line: It's not environment or genetics. It's a choice. Yeah, there are definitely things that happen to people that have them totally hurt and looking for relief. Abuse, being used and exploited by people they love, or even being abandoned. There are so many things that destroy people's hope and security, which could send them searching for an answer through destructive decisions and lifestyles, but they are all to cover up something, to fill a void, or in hope that being gay will give you happiness. None of these will ever work.

Most overused and annoying quote about homosexuality:

"God created Adam and Eve, not Adam and Steve."

1+0=Gay?

> *I'm a dude and, well, I'm not attracted to girls at all, so I guess I must be gay.*
> —comment made by a high school junior

It's a gay lie. People who are not attracted to the opposite sex get put in the "must be queer" pressure cooker, where they are seasoned and basted in gay rhetoric until they finally emerge as a flaming piece of converted meat.

If this is you, you know exactly what I am talking about. Everyone tries to convince you that there is no other option—if you don't like the opposite sex, you must be gay. No. Wrong. Stop. You're not gay, and there *are* other options.

Have you ever thought about the fact that God may have some way cool things he needs you to do and he, with all his God-smarts, knows that if you get wrapped up in the hormone shuffle, you will totally miss out on what he has for you? Listen, you are not gay just because you aren't chasing hotties. God has something for you. Quit listening to all the "ya gotta get crushin'" crap and get excited that you don't have to hook up with anyone to be complete. Start looking at your options. See where God is taking you.

Life is a blast. Get to living it. Major things in this world have happened because of people who were rollin' solo. Don't be afraid of a crush, but please don't be afraid to keep it single. It doesn't make you gay. If you want to get spiritual about it, then let's take a look and see what God says to those people who say, "Just go for it. It's natural." Read 1 Corinthians 6:9; Romans 1:24–27; Leviticus 18:22. God makes it clear that homosexuality is not an option. Hey, my girlfriend and I have the urge to sex it up, but just because we have an urge doesn't mean we do it. Fight the urge. Don't buy the lie. 🐾

Myth #398

• • •

I have had thoughts and dreams about people of the same sex, so I must be gay.

Gurl2Gurl

You may be one of those girls out there who just likes to be with girls. I mean, you are a girl, and you get along better with other girls. You have more in common with them than you do guys. They are easier to talk to, and you connect with them on a deeper level. And all of this makes you feel wonderful, and . . . omg! You must be gay. Right?

Listen, this is all cool stuff. But none of it makes you gay. Getting along better with girls doesn't make you gay, it makes you . . . oh, what's the word . . . it's another g-word . . . it makes you . . . oh yeah, a *GIRL!*

Of course you connect better with girls. Hello! You have way more in common with them. Listen, I would much rather hang out with the fellas than I would a bunch of girls. Especially with guys who are into basketball. We have so much more in common. We connect even more when we play ball together. That doesn't mean I'm going to switch teams 'cause I'm gay. Even when I slap a dude on the butt for making a good play, I am not acting out some suppressed desire that wants out. I mean, what else am I suppose to do, slap him upside the head?

We get along with people who are into the same stuff and who have had similar experiences. Usually that's people of the same sex. It's not being gay, it's being a girl.

Dream
ANALYSIS

You're not gay. You're normal. Everyone has had some kind of thought about the same sex. It may have been a quick thought, or it may have made you stop and wonder. Either way, it's just that—a thought.

Here's the prob. In today's society we are telling people they need to latch onto that thought and explore it. Let it come out. It may be some repressed identity trying to get out. Or it could be the Mexican food. Whatever!

Don't ponder it. Just let it go. I can see a girl walking down the street and think, "Dang! She's hot!" and just keep on walking without going through this sex-romp in my mind, and nothing is wrong with that. It was just a thought. It flew in, flew out. It's gone. The problem comes when people try to get you to latch onto the thoughts and really explore them. This burns the image on your mind, and if you do this enough, your mind will start believing it. It is not because your being gay is coming out. It is because you have talked yourself into being gay because of what your mind continued to think about.

Again, if you have had those kinds of thoughts, you are not some freak-o or gay. You are normal. Sure, you'll find those who will try to tell you that they have never, ever thought something like that. They are under the clinical classification of *lying*. So don't worry about it. But don't expect all the guys on the team to sit around and talk about it! 🐾

Myth #81

• • •

My penis
is too small.

Big Man

on

Campus

American males have a major hang-up about the size of their goods. It has always been a male concern, but the issue has become a cancer eroding the self-confidence of men.

The reason for the increase in penile preoccupation is the accessibility of pornography. If a guy gets into the pornographic fantasy photos, before long he thinks he's inadequate because he doesn't have a third leg. These pictures are not the real world, yet they are another way that the Enemy is destroying the image that God has given men of themselves.

Reality is, and the studies confirm, that penis size is **not an issue to anyone except men** worried about what their friends say in the locker room. It is not a sign of manhood, of power, or even of how much you will be able to satisfy your future wife.

So realize, God made you. He picked you out to be exactly like you are. Your eyes, your hair, how tall you are, the way you laugh. Even your penis size. He put all of this together and made you like you are 'cause he thought this was the coolest combination ever. You are you, and he made you exactly right.

So don't sweat the small stuff. (Sorry!) 🐛

Penile P.S.: Here's a last thought about the size of your business. What if God made your penis the exact size that it is so that it will be perfectly compatible with your wife? Hmm?

The Making of a Man

Mr. Wannabe Rapper says: "Oralizing and sexizing the honeys makes you the manizzle with the fazzizzle."

Translation: Having oral sex and regular sex with girls makes you a real man.

Actually, Mr. Izzle, this belief will take you far from your destiny of manhood, unless your manhood involves handing all your man-dom over to a girlie by dropping your pants and waiting to see if she'll laugh at you.

When you expect sex (regular, oral, whatever) to make you feel like a man or look like a man with your friends, what you have done is given your manhood to that girl. Her acceptance and reaction to you will determine if you feel like a man. Even if your "Ug! I am man!" test is passed and you can tell all your buds about your sexcapade, you have made a girl the maker of your manhood, and that is impossible.

Newsflash to the naïve: Your manhood cannot come from sexing the ladies. It cannot come from what other guys say about you. This man vibe is all about you and something way bigger than you: God.

ULTIMATE MALE ENHANCEMENT SECRETS

You wanna be a man? A real man? The first thing you need to do is stop trying to be a man. 'Cause you can't. Check it. You were created male. That came automatic. But the Creator wants to make you a man. *God* is where your manhood is. Guys look everywhere else trying to find it. Sports. Women. Violence. Anywhere they can feel like they have what it takes. But the source of all manness is the Source of everything.

So how do you get it? How do you access this vault of man-stuff?

Ask

In the letter James wrote, he laid it out pretty clear. In the fourth chapter he wrote, "You do not have, because you do not ask God." The one who created you has all these man things he wants to give you, but the key is, you have to ask. He wants you to depend on him and know that you can get anything from him if you ask. That way you know it came from him. So start asking God to make you a real man, and don't stop asking until you get all the vibe he's got.

Now, there is a catch to all this. Of course, there's always a catch. James put it down like this: "When you ask, you do not receive, because you ask with wrong motives, that you may spend what you get on your pleasures." Ouch-o-rama. God wants you to have everything. But he's not going to make you a real man if you want it so you can hook up with hotter honeys or so that you can go beat up the football QB. It's all about the motives.

So what's the right answer here? God wants to give you his entire arsenal of manness for one reason only: so that you will honor him with it. What does that mean in the real world? I can't tell you. It's different for everyone.

Remember David in the Bible? God started giving David his manhood when he was just a kid out doing the shepherd thing. He would sit around, play the harp, sing praises to God. He was way sensitive. He would cry anytime something happened to his sheep. But he wasn't a wuss. God gave him his man vibe. David killed a lion and a bear with his bare hands. That was God giving him even more manhood. Why? 'Cause there was a giant that God needed to have killed. David was still a teen, but he used his manhood to honor God.

Okay, so, if you are going to be a man, you have to start asking for it from the only one who can give it to you. Then what?

Pray

Every day, connect with God. Talk to him. Tell him exactly what you think and feel. Admit your weakness and that you can't do it on your own. This isn't about pansyness. It's about plugging into the source of all power. Check out Paul, the dude who wrote a lot of the New Testament. He was a man. He went through beatings, shipwrecks, snake bites, prison. He was tough. But listen to what he said in his second letter to the Corinthians: "When I am weak, then I am strong" (chapter 12, verse 10). He knew he was weak. He knew that on his own, he could not do anything. And he also knew where the strength was—God. So start connecting with God as much as possible.

One word on prayer: Don't let anyone tell you there is only one way to pray. Everyone has a different way. God is creative. He doesn't talk to everyone in exactly the same way. So get some books or tapes or talk with your youth pastor. Find some different ways to pray. And remember, if your prayer life is boring, it's not because prayer is boring, it's because the method you are using doesn't jive with the way God made you. So find a new way.

Get the Word

This doesn't mean go get a Bible, unless you don't have one. But lots of people with Bibles still don't have all the manhood God wants for them. Why? 'Cause they haven't really gotten into the Word. This means read it. Study it. Check out what is going on.

So many people try to get into reading the Bible and quit 'cause they say, "I just can't understand it." And you know what? You can't. So if you are thinking that you are going to figure out what the Bible is saying without the help of the Holy Spirit, give it up. Check it in 1 Corinthians, the second chapter, verses 6 through 16. It's all there. Go find one of those Holy Bibles and read it. Verse 14 makes it Casper clear: "The man without the Spirit does not accept the things that come from the Spirit of God, for they are foolishness to him, and he cannot understand them, because they are spiritually discerned." Connect that to what Luke wrote in his historical account of Jesus' life: "He opened their eyes so they could understand the Scriptures" (24:45). Click those two together and break it down to electron level. You will never understand the things of God on your own. The Spirit of the Almighty has to reveal it to you. The Word of God is, well, a thing of God. So you will not understand it until the Holy Spirit reveals it to you.

So the big Q now is, "How can I get this stuff 'revealed' to me?" Read on . . .

Who's Your Christ?

All of these things are revealed by the Spirit of God. This Holy Spirit that is in God needs to be in you. How? When you accept Jesus as the sacrifice for all your sins and make him the ruler of your life, God sends his Spirit into you. If you have done this, great! If you haven't, see the section, "Got God?" 'Cause nothing else will connect for you until that does.

Ask to Know

Check Psalm 119. It has verse after verse of the author, a God-connected man, asking the Almighty to show his meaning of the words. God wants you to know, but sometimes you have to ask for it. Dig for it. Search for the meaning. Again, ask and don't stop until you get it.

Learn It

Remember, we are not talking about being a good-little-churchy-guy. We are still talking about your manhood. Time for a rousing game of connect the dots.

Psalms chapter 66 verse 18 says, "If I had cherished sin in my heart, the Lord would not have listened." Now if God's not listening, he probably ain't talking either.

Psalms chapter 119 verse 11 says, "I have hidden your word in my heart that I might not sin against you."

Now, who holds your manhood and is dying to give it to you? Yep, God.

So connect the dots here. If we sin, we are cut off from the Source of our manhood. And God cannot give us what we desperately want. So what can we do to help us stay connected?

Keep up now. Here we go.

I memorize Scripture so I will not sin against God

The Scripture in my heart will help me not to sin

I will stay connected to God

God is the Source of my manhood

He can give me my manhood

Do you smell what we're cooking here? Memorizing Scripture does not make you a man. But it will help you stay connected to the Source. And if you are connected, his Holy Spirit can reveal to you how to get your manhood. And that's power, baby!

Get Churchin'

I know, I've heard all the excuses for not getting connected with a church group. It's boring. I don't get anything from it. It's a bunch of geeks. I've heard it all. In fact, I have probably said it all.

But here's the way it works. Church is what you make it. Yeah, it's cliché, but it's true. I always hated Sunday morning church. Way too early and way too boring. I started going to Sunday school (I hate that word too!) at a church only to find more of the same—except that it was full of motorheads. There were pro race car drivers. Pro and pro-am motocross racers. Some off-road junkies.

And then all the other people associated with that kind of stuff. Mechanics, car haulers, fans. We all got together and decided that if this was our class, then we were going to do it our way. And man, did things change. We had tires stacked in the corner. Mufflers, motor parts, and steering wheels hanging from the ceiling. There was a mini sprint car coming out of the wall. It was wild. It was unlike anything anyone ever expected, especially at this church, and we loved going. We couldn't wait to get there Sunday mornings.

The point of all this is that if the church you're going to is boring, it's 'cause you are letting it be boring. Don't just quit going. Do something. The church is where you are going to find other warriors fighting for their manhood. And with a band of brothers fighting together, it is a battle you will win.

This was a long answer for a short question, but it is one of the most important questions a guy will ever face. **And here's a little bonus.** If you want to kick your manhood into hyper-speed, then check out a book called *Wild at Heart* by John Eldredge. It will blow you away. Another incredible book that is a must-have is called *Dateable: Are You? Are They?* by Justin Lookadoo and Hayley Morgan. (Shameless self-promotion. You gotta love it.) Scope out the Man Vibe sections in *Dateable*.

Herpes

The Greek God of Blisters and Deception

Herpes is the master of infiltrating enemies without their knowledge. He displays great characteristics of stealth and deception.

Utilizing human carelessness and naïveté, Herpes entrenches himself into the body of one person. Then, patiently, he waits for an opening in the skin or for the bodily fluid of his current slave to come into contact with another unsuspecting victim. This is the bridge which allows him to move undetected and continue to conquer.

Once he has infected the new host, he waits 2–30 days before showing symptoms of his presence. When he does allow himself to be noticed, it is with flulike symptoms and small painful blisters on the genital area. He stays out in the open harassing, irritating, and causing pain for 1 to 3 weeks. Then he goes back underground, where he again waits.

His deceptive tactics are demonstrated most clearly during the times of symptomless silence. The conquered land in which he is living often believes that when the sores go away, they are free of their tormentor. **But, alas, they will never be free.** Once Herpes seizes a new land, a new life, it will have to endure his wrath forever.

Herpes is a conquering nomad. He could never be satisfied with being confined to a single place. He has to expand his territory and control. One of the best ways he does this is by convincing the host that when they don't feel or see visible sores, they cannot pass Herpes to another. The host is tricked into believing they always know when the symptoms are active. But this is an illusion, a false sense of security, because Herpes is ready to move on even during times when the sores are not seen or even felt. And then Herpes is able to conquer and destroy another life through the help of an unwilling partner.

Through the years medications have been developed to help suppress the symptoms of the Greek god Herpes. But nothing has been able to cure him once he has entered the body he has conquered.

Myth #27

• • •

Condoms prevent pregnancy and diseases.

Nothing
to Lose

If this stuff doesn't relate to you, then skip it. Don't just keep reading and then whine about how it didn't relate. Go away. But if it does relate, read on.

Odds are that one out of every 5 people reading this book right now has some kind of STD. No, not because of this book, dork. But we know the odds because that's what the expert-type people tell us.

Some obvious stages of freaking out come with the news. Shock. Sadness. Depression. Embarrassment. Anger. These are normal reactions. Some people I have talked to don't process through the issues, and they stop in the rage stage. They don't bounce back when they hit bottom. Instead they stick there like gum on the bottom of your shoe. They get bitter and want revenge, or, even more commonly, they feel like they are worthless now, so they might as well go out and have more sex. And why worry about protection—I mean, what's gonna happen, you're gonna catch a disease? Too late.

That's trauma talk. True, if you have something like herpes, HPV, or HIV, you will not get rid of it. But **your life is not over.** The disease is now a part of your makeup. But it's time to deal and get back to living. Don't let it become your identity. There are some things you can do to keep your life going.

First, go to the doc. They can give you some meds to control the stuff. Then get to a counselor. Let them help you deal with the shock and work through the depression, the feelings of dirtiness, and all the other emotional junk.

Listen, the Enemy is going to tell you that you are nasty, damaged goods. That's not the truth. Jesus died for this kind of stuff. Understand that the reason he was nailed to the cross was to take your sins with him. The sex, the herpes, the lies. He came for all that stuff. Satan will get in your head and tell you that you're worthless. Wrong. All lies from the pit of hell. You are still the most valuable thing God has ever created. That's the way he sees you. You may not feel like it, but it's true.

Don't be scared to run to God. He knows what has happened. Tell him. Clear the air. He doesn't expect you to be totally perfect, but he expects you to be totally honest. Confess what you've done and then thank him for his forgiveness. Picture all that stuff nailed to the cross. And when those thoughts of how horrible you are come to your mind, just say out loud, "Nope, that is nailed to the cross." And leave it there.

One more little thought:

I know you will feel a lot of anger if you catch a disease. You will hate the person who gave it to you. Sometimes people decide the best way to deal is to get back at other people by sexing them, knowing that it could give them a disease. I know that sounds twisted, but some think they have nothing to lose and so if they are going down, they are going to take some jerks with them. They think, hey, some people just use girls or just mess with people's lives, and they deserve it. No. Nobody deserves it. You didn't deserve it. And no one, no matter what they have done, deserves it. And this could backfire. Check the reals on it. You could give it to some jerk because you think he deserves it. He sleeps with a girl who hooks up with this dude who starts going out with your best friend, and in a moment of weakness, she has sex with him. Now she has it. You just gave herpes to your best friend. She didn't deserve it. And neither did you.

Don't let me lie. This is going to be a tough journey. But you don't have to do it alone. Get some major bud support and adult help, and remember, Christ is there waiting for you to ask him to jump in and help. Ask. 𝒟

Sowhatta-yaknow?

_____ syphilis

_____ chlamydia

_____ HPV (genital warts)

_____ herpes

_____ HIV

_____ gonorrhea

Answers: 5, 2, 1, 3, 6, 4

The above white space is courtesy of the book designer, who has become a little oatmeal brained after making it this far through the book. He is hopeful the space will give you a nice little breather before continuing on.

A a a a h h h h h h h h ... that's nice.

3 Myths

Discussed Intelligently and Adultlike

(without the use of the following phrases: "terminally stupid," "do you know you're an idiot?" "you poopie-head," and "when do your moron meds run out?")

> Myth #203
>
> • • •
>
> **Masturbating means you are a lonely, twisted perv.**

How terminally stupid! (Oops, we already blew it. . . . We tried.)

Some say that 95% of males have masturbated and the other 5% are lying. I don't know if that is true 'cause I haven't been peeking in your windows.

But here's the big battle Q: **"Is masturbation wrong?"** Man, I can't find anything that speaks directly to it in Scripture. But it says lots of things about controlling your thoughts and lust.

So to impart my infinite wisdom on the question of, "Is it okay? Can people masturbate?" let me dip deeper into my shallow pool of intelligence. Here is my take on the whole deal.

For some people masturbation becomes a major prob because it becomes a habit. You can get addicted to it just like anything else because it gives your brain a rush. A bunch of feel-good chemicals are shot into the brain, and people get addicted to that feeling. They get to the point that they have to do it. It's all they can think about. They have to leave class or a party, or, well, anytime the urge hits, they have to go do it. It controls them.

If you are reading this and laughing, I am not talking to you. If you're sitting there and this sounds familiar, it's time to take back your life. And the first step is, grab an adult you really trust and tell it! This will be the hardest thing you have ever done, but you have to. Right now you have all this stuff hidden in the dark. And that is prime growth time for it. Shine light on it, and it cannot survive or control you. Sin is like a bunch of roaches. In the darkness, they get everywhere. But flip the switch, and it's every roach for himself as he scrambles away.

After you do that, get a plan. Talk with your youth pastor or a counselor. You need to control yourself, so find someone who won't let you lie to yourself anymore. You have to do it. It's a battle for your soul.

Now what about those who are not controlled by masturbation? Well, for you the question is this: What's going on in your brain? What are your thoughts doing? The guide we are to use for our life tells us in the Book of Matthew, the 5th chapter and the 28th verse, "But I tell you that anyone who looks at a woman lustfully has already committed adultery with her in his heart." This is not an eye issue. It's a brain issue. And the verse is pretty clear.

Masturbation has a sex connection. The Bible is clear on the boundaries of sex itself, but like I said, it doesn't say anything specific about this. So this might be classified as a gray area. And anytime you get into this kind of gray area, you have to be careful. So that means where you and sex are concerned, even masturbation can be dangerous territory.

Look at the real issue: God wants you to have self-control

Go Ask Grandpa!

Grandpa, I heard that masturbating will make hair grown on your palms. Is that true?

Son, why do you think I wear gloves all the time? (Heh, heh!) . . . No, really, that ain't true. Back when I was in the army, I heard all that stuff. It would grow hair on your palms, make you go blind, make you go insane. All kinds of things. But if that were true, there would have been a bunch of blind, hairy-palmed, crazy soldiers running around . . . uh . . . wait, come to think of it, maybe it was true. Naw, I'm just kidding with you. Now go get your Grandpa some applesauce.

and a pure mind and to become all he made you to be. Rather than obsessing about whether you can find chapter and verse of the Bible to tell you whether masturbation is right or wrong, ask yourself, "Does it control me?" and "What's going on in my mentals?" Answer those questions honestly. No, really, *honestly.*

Lots more could be said about the subject. But we don't have the time or space to cover it all here. If you need more info, talk to someone you trust about it—or you can even email me with your questions. But for now, that's all I got.

Myth #21

• • •

The doctor can tell if you've had sex or not.

The hymen is the question here. It's a fold of tissue that partly covers the entrance to the vagina of a virgin and is broken at the first sexual contact. Right? Well, yes and no. The hymen is real. But it tears for lots of reasons other than sex. It could tear from using a tampon, from stretching, from rollerblading, or maybe for no real reason at all. So just the fact that the hymen is not intact does not mean the girl has had sex.

That is the physical answer to the question. But you need to understand that virginity is more emotional and spiritual than physical. Sex creates a soul connection between two people. It's not really a physical barrier but rather a spiritual-emotional barrier of protection that sex breaks through. All of a sudden, with sex, you are exposed to rejection, hurt, and insecurities like never before.

So can a doctor tell if you have had sex? Physically, no. But I have talked to several doctors who say they can tell. It's because teens they have known since they were little kids start acting weird. Not just teen weirdness but majorly depressed and emotional, and their self-esteem is shot. And they are not into drugs. In fact, Dr. Meg Meeker says, "At pediatric conferences many of my colleagues report the same thing: increased post-traumatic stress disorder in sexually active teens." So if your doc is in tune with the real world and has known you a while, they will probably be able to tell.

Myth #132

• • •

You can't get pregnant or get an STD if you do it fast or if he doesn't stick it in all the way.

Yeah, and I won't die if I get run over by a truck as long as the truck is going *really* fast. Pssst. Here's a secret. The speed of the truck is *not* the issue. The problem happens when the truck comes in contact with your face.

Stupid Simplistic Translation: As soon as any skin or fluid from one person comes in contact with another, you have the potential "Oh no" outcome. It doesn't matter how fast or how slow you do it or how quick you clean it off; it's about the point of contact. Doing it just once could cause disease or pregnancy. It's all a gamble. And you are betting your life!

Restroom wisdom

(So why would we snoop around restrooms waiting for juicy morsels of Dirt? We're hungry. And they kicked us out of the Y.)

I'm not gonna like it!

We asked a male of the species to comment on this restroom wisdom.

My wife had better enjoy sex! If she doesn't, we must be doing something wrong. God made sex, and he said it was good. If it wasn't, no one would do it. So a married woman should enjoy it. She should get into it, experiment, get freaky, have fun.

Now before you run off and say we told you to go have sex and enjoy, understand that he is talking about married couples. Right?!

Oh, yeah. It will mess up the system if you get into sex without the marriage. But once you're there, sex is not a bad thing. It's all good.

(Shameless plug for the other lonely chapters of this book: If you want to enjoy sex to the max, then wait. See ULTIMATE SEX FORMULA REVEALED on page 95.)

No Skanks for Me, Please.

Clueless Proof Question: So if *they* don't know they have something, how are *you* going to know? What, just because they look healthy and act healthy, they must *be* healthy?

Hottie with a Body . . .
and a Little Bit More

I was blown away one night in a men's Bible study. All us dudes were just sitting around doing our thing when a guy began to talk. He was big, tall, good-looking. Hey, I'm secure enough in my manhood to tell you he was *hot.* He had one of those bodies like on the front of mags, with the washboard stomach, strong jawline, killer smile. And he had the personality to go with it. He was the package.

This dude broke down crying in the middle of everyone. He told us that he didn't think that he would ever find anyone to love him because he has herpes. Okay, *that* was not what we were expecting. This guy was the poster child for health and happiness, but he will have that disease for the rest of his life.

Rupert the Fact-Finding Ferret says:

Get a grip on these factoids.
-- 80% of people who have STDs don't even know they are infected.
-- 2/3 of infections are spread by people with no identifiable symptoms.

This factoid moment has been brought to you by the smart people who wrote the Washington State University Microbiology Internet Text. (They make ferrets do all their work.)

The Gift of the Frog Prince

Once upon a time a young princess found a frog prince. He was cute, in a slimy amphibian sort of way. So she decided to break his spell and kissed him. Poof! This slimy frog turned into a hottie of a prince. He was tall and handsome and wanted more than just a kiss. With some sweet talk about love and a future together, she finally gave in. I mean, why not? He's a prince, after all. Not some dirty ol' toad.

Her time with the prince was beautiful, and she was glowing with love as she watched her prince ride off into the sunset. Then, to her surprise, between 1 and 6 months after they had sex, she received her first of many outbreaks of HPV, also known as genital warts. (What else would you catch from a frog prince?) With this gift of love came small, bumpy warts on her sex organs and anus. It also brings itching and burning down there.

And as a remembrance of her youthful encounter, she gets to keep these warts as long as she lives, because there is no cure. She couldn't believe this had happened to her until she learned from the Kaiser Family Foundation that there are more than 5 million new cases every year.

Every once in a while the maiden sees the prince down at the royal clinic. Here they pick up topical cream and sometimes have liquid nitrogen applied to freeze the warts off. Sometimes they have surgical procedures to remove wart clusters, and yet at other times they don't have any symptoms at all. But that doesn't mean it's gone, because they will live their lives wartfully ever after.

Myth #216

...

If you caught an STD, you might as well have unprotected sex 'cause you've got nothing to lose.

The ULTIMATE Sex Formula Revealed

The secret of great sex has been discovered and now is available directly to you. In the midst of breast enlargement cream, virility spray, and every kind of male enhancement supplement you can imagine, the ULTIMATE sex formula has been discovered, and we are giving it to you FREE for your personal use.

Basic Formula

1 male + 1 female x 1 marriage commitment
= Great Sex

Advanced Formula

1 virgin male + 1 virgin female x 1 marriage commitment
= ULTIMATE Sex

Yes, that's right. According to research reported by Glenn T. Staton in *Why Marriage Matters Series: No 2,* the people who are most satisfied with their sex lives are not the unmarried sex fiends but rather the married couples. And the very most sex satisfaction was reported by those who were virgins when they married.

So the ULTIMATE sexual enhancement secret is to wait. Hold off on the sex games until you are married, and then get ready for the ULTIMATE SEXUAL EXPERIENCE.

S Survey ays...

Do teens wish they had waited for sex?

In the name of scientific discovery, ancient wisdom, and the lack of any friends, we went on a quest to find out if sex was really all that good and why. After many hours of fact-finding research, numerous slaps in the face, and a couple of restraining orders, we decided to take a more sensible approach and ask some experts. They wouldn't take our calls even though we disguised our voices (*drat that caller ID!*), so we took to the Internet. And did we find some juicy stuff.

According to the National Campaign to Prevent Teen Pregnancy, somewhere between 67 and 81% of teens who have had sex wish they had waited. That's a bunch of second-thoughters.

To get a clear pic on the truth, go back to the digs in Calling All Virgins, where it was reported that about ½ of all teens have had sex and ½ have not. Put these pieces together and see what the puzzle looks like. And since I am a visual learner, I will insert graph here:

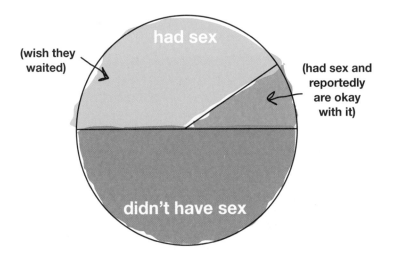

(wish they waited)

had sex

(had sex and reportedly are okay with it)

didn't have sex

Why such a small clique of sexually giddy teens? Well, we found the answer with the coolest doc we've ever met. Her name is Dr. Meg Meeker. She has been doing the doctor thing for a long time, and she has studied the deal on what sex really does to teens.

She said that the mambo-reason (that's doc talk for big reason) for the intercourse blues is what she calls Emotional STDs. So we decided to hit some of the most contagious and dangerous of the E-STDs.

Depression

The biggest emotional side effect of teen sex is depression. So what does that mean? Depression is just the label they give to some negative spice happening inside of somebody at a core level. Of course, if you are like me, you'd have to eat with plastic spoons for your own protection.

and also, you'd ask if this whole sex/depression connection thing was really a bunch of made-up poopie-scoop to scare teens into not having sex. But hey, it is so real that Doc Meg says, "I screen all sexually active teens for depression." *All* of them. It's that real.

In fact, The Heritage Foundation just came out with some super-sexed info. They found that there was a direct A + B = C connection between teen sex and depression. They also said there was a major connection between teen sex and suicide. This stuff is real. And it is a real hot-zone of destruction.

Rejection

Sex opens a person up to major rejection. You are totally exposed physically, emotionally, and spiritually. The other person can destroy you in an instant—especially if you are not in a committed, secure marriage.

Check it. When people get into sex, they get vulnerable. They are looking for acceptance. They are hoping to know that they can satisfy someone else and in doing so get an ego boost so they can like themselves more. But look. You have two people who are not totally committed to helping the other become what God wants them to be. You throw your clothes off in passion fashion, and then the dude looks at you and says, "What are those dimples?

Is that cellulite?" or "I thought your boobs were bigger."
Or flip the script. Fellas, you are all about knowing you
are a real man, and you will prove it by sexing this hottie. In your most manly and primal way, you drop your
pants, and she *giggles.* Or before you can even start the
sexing, oops, you're finished. These are just a few of the
things that could happen that would put you in overdrive
on the rejection highway.

Betrayal This E-STD is a killer of teens, of friendships, and of lives,
and it happens in many ways. The most popular passing of
this unpopular E-STD is when someone opens themselves
up to this intimate sexual moment expecting the other person to honor and protect what happened between them.
Then the next day at school, people are chatting about it.
And instantly you know it's not just some rumor because
people are talking specifics. Yeah, you are going to feel
betrayed. And a piece of you will be ripped apart.

Another betrayal infection zone is the love 'em and
leave 'em. You hear about this way too often. After dating
each other for a while, two people are getting closer and
closer to each other. Everything is going smoothly, so they
decide to do what they *think* is naturally the next step,
and they have sex. Almost instantly one of them (usually

the guy) freaks out and bounces the relationship. The girl is left with the guilt and hurt, feeling totally betrayed . . . because she was!

Guilt

Most of the time guilt is a natural side effect of doing something wrong. And with sex comes a buffet of guilt possibilities. The guilt of exposing yourself and giving a piece of you to someone not committed to you. The guilt of going against God. The guilt associated with the parentals' disappointment.

Don't get confused, though. Guilt is not necessarily bad. 'Cause it has a purpose. Guilt is supposed to make you stop and think about what you are doing and what is really going on. But two major negative vibes can also happen when guilt comes:

Guilt-a-thon: The Enemy is going to try to keep reminding you over and over that you messed up. He is going to tell you that God doesn't love you as much anymore because you are damaged goods. Listen, that is Satan trying to get in your head and destroy you. Why do you think Paul told us to put on the helmet of salvation? He knew that Satan would attack our mentals.

When you have dealt with the mess-up—you have told it to God and let him forgive you—it's done. So when the after-guilt comes, just stop and focus on God. Don't fight the guilty feelings, because that means you are giving them attention. Don't. Just focus on God and tell him some of the things that are so cool about him.

Guilt-shield: Another major prob is when people finally stop feeling the guilt. Some people will tell you to quit being a baby or that the guilt will go away pretty soon and everything will be okay. And it's true, you can become numb to the guilt. But that doesn't mean everything is okay. In fact, it's worse. Then you become like someone who has no feeling in his hand and has it sitting on a hot stove. Just because he doesn't feel the pain doesn't mean everything is okay. In fact, when the yuck of the wound starts in, the pain and problems will be even worse. Just because you have stopped feeling guilty about sex doesn't mean it's all good. It means when it finally blows up, your wounded heart and emotions will be nasty-infected.

Insecurity

There is no way you can get into the teen sex thing and be totally secure. On the relationship anatomy chart, the most basic building block that all things sexual are dependent on is a total acceptance and commitment—that means marriage. And with the whole marriage thing, you don't belong to yourself anymore. You belong to your spouse, and your spouse belongs to you. Not in some sweatshop-slave-labor kind of way. It's more of a straight-up "take me, I'm yours" vibe. There is ownership to the commitment. Outside of marriage it is more like a rental.

Sex Rental Breakdown

Everyone knows that people treat rental cars like crap. Why? Because it's not theirs. It doesn't belong to them. So they'll run over anything. Curbs. Road trash. Small circus ponies. Anything. They will get in some two-door, match-box-sized economy car and drive it like it's a mixed breed of NASCAR racer and monster truck. Plus, people rent cars they would never, ever own. They use the car for the amount of time they need it, turn it in, and walk away.

A rental actually costs a lot more than the car you own. Run it: Say a rental costs $50 per day. So you rent it for 30 days. Your monthly car payment is $1500. So every time you get in a rental, it's a high-ticket investment.

Sex Rental Translation

Sex without marriage is like a rental car. People will use you. Drive you around. And then, it's no problem to get rid of you. Why? 'Cause there's no commitment. No ownership.

Yeah, during the relationship it seems like there is a lot of value, a lot being invested. But they just turn and walk. It's easy.

And realize that just like people rent a car they would never buy, many people will date and have sex with folks they would never marry.

Value comes with ownership. Ownership comes with marriage. You can never feel secure if you are a rental.

Everyone wants to marry a virgin, you just don't want to date one.

—a high school philosopher

Letdown Factor

Another part of teen sex is the letdown factor. Society and the media set us up for sexual failure. We are promised so many things attached to sex. Excitement, passion, beauty, fulfillment. But for most of the people I talk with, sex is more of a letdown. Disappointing, embarrassing, unfulfilling.

The problem is that a lot of people connect the wrong dots. When they hit the sex scene, they know there is something wrong. But instead of thinking there is something wrong with having sex without the ownership of marriage like they are, they think there must be something wrong with them. So they keep going to sex over and over again, trying to fix what is wrong with them each time. But every time they get the same result. They never stop and think, "Maybe it's the sex, not me." This solidifies their insecurity and feeds their depression.

And one more note: If sex was like they portray it on TV, the world would stop. Everyone would be at home by the fire making love until noon. Wrong answer.

Devaluation

Let's get all chromosomal for a minute. Humanoids are made with an automatic need to protect the body. It is valuable and thought of as important, if nothing more than because it houses stuff like kidneys, hearts, and brains. Some important stuff. So there is a natural instinct to guard the body.

When sex happens and it is just a casual thing, an automatic devaluation starts happening. The body is exposed and used, and the mind has to do something. Here was this body that was supposed to be a prized possession, and it was loaned out for the pleasure of others. So the mind assumes that the value of the body must have been lowered. This way the mind can justify that the value matches the actions. And the twisted part about all this is that a lot of people start making decisions that trash their life, and they don't know why. They tell everyone that it's just what they want to do. But really it's because they see themselves as trash, so they start treating themselves like trash.

God disconnect

Getting into the sex scene totally disconnects you from God. It's not because he runs away from you or he hates you. It's because you walk away from him. He hasn't moved. His anointed Scripture tells us that he is constant. He is the same yesterday, today, and forever. So what happens is that when you get into sex, you turn your back on God. And you can't face two directions at one time. It is physically and spiritually impossible.

So it's up to you. You can continue living outside of what God has said and miss out on what he wants to give you. Or you can reconnect with him and let him start working through all the issues with you and giving you all the goods he has for you.

Emotional STDs are real. They can be even more dangerous and destructive than the physical stuff. They affect millions more people than all the physical STDs combined. If you are going through this stuff, know that it will be hard. You will have to wade through the crap and the quicksand and get to the other side. But you can do it. Stay close to the Creator, who is still there waiting on you. And you will come through this stronger than ever.

Myth #326

...

If I get pregnant
I will go ahead and finish school, and my life will **go on as planned.**

No Going Back

I've already messed up and had sex. Does that mean my life is ruined? Help! —Rachel B., 16

Absolutely not! Your life is not ruined. You'll never be able to undo what you did, that's for sure. It would be like if you went skydiving. Once you did it, you would never be able to undo it. But this is one thing in your life. Just like skydiving will not totally change or trash your life (unless you crash), this one incident will not be your every thought and control your life unless you crashed (pregnancy or disease). If you were fortunate enough to walk away relatively unharmed, it's time to keep walking.

Realize that you are probably going to have some issues to get through. You're going to have to face God. You're going to have to get the forgiveness vibe flowing. You're going to have to remember that virginity is more about the spiritual and emotional than the physical. Run to God.

. . . Okay, wait. I was about to give you several little feel-good churchy clichés that would sound good but wouldn't really do anything for you. Instead, let's get to the dirt of how to get through this.

Break it down. You had sex. Now it has clicked in that you're messed up. How are you gonna deal?

But remember this—the wrong desires that come into your life aren't anything new and different. Many others have faced exactly the same problems before you. And no temptation is irresistible. You can trust God to keep the temptation from becoming so strong that you can't stand up against it, for he has promised this and will do what he says. He will show you how to escape temptation's power so that you can bear up patiently against it.

—the apostle Paul,
1 Cor. ten:thirteen TLB

Pray. This is the part between you and God. Tell him all about it. Paul the apostle let us know that with temptation, God gives us a way out, and all we have to do is take it. So admit to God where you totally ignored your way out. Take a deep breath, shut your eyes, and tell him exactly what you feel. Or if you connect better by writing, write out your prayer. Tell God you are truly sorry and you need him to forgive you. If you've never prayed before or are not sure you're on good terms with God, go read "Got God?" and make sure you're set.

Jesus died for this stuff. You need to understand that. So here's what you are going to do. You are going to use your imagination. You are going to close your eyes and walk up to the cross. You can see Jesus on it or just the cross, whatever works for you. I want you to walk up to it with a piece of paper in your hand. On that piece of paper is all the stuff you feel awful about. All the things that you did to let yourself down, to let God down, everything. Walk up to the cross and nail that piece of paper to the cross. That's what Jesus died for. So do it. It won't take long.

Now leave it there. I say that 'cause the Enemy is going to try to tell you that you are damaged goods and that's the way God sees you. When these thoughts come, say out loud, "No! I nailed that to the cross." And see in your mind the paper nailed to the cross.

Accept forgiveness. Yeah, God has forgiven you, so it's time for you to accept it.

When you refuse to accept it and say, "I just can't forgive myself," you are holding yourself to a higher standard than God holds you to, as if he isn't good enough for you. Don't get all martyr-dramatic here. It won't make him forgive you any more, 'cause he's already forgiven it all. It's done.

You may think you deserve to be punished or that you are worthless. And in a sense you probably are, because we all are. Hey, I'm not calling you out, that's what it says in Romans six:twenty-three, *"For all have sinned and fallen short of the glory of God."* None of us deserves to be alive because we are so sinful. But don't make light of Christ's death on the cross, as if it wasn't enough to cover your sins. That's what he died for. You're not such a horrible, tragic case that you just can't be forgiven by God. Don't act as if he isn't big enough. He is. Accept it.

Let go of the blame.

If you are spreading blame and holding bitterness for what happened, then guess what—it's time to let it go. First thing you have to do is figure out who you need to forgive. Who is it? The person you had sex with? Your parents? I don't know, maybe you blame them for letting you do it. God? Jot down all the people you are ticked off at or upset with. Anyone you think you need to stop blaming.

Okay, you are about to pray to get rid of the junk that you're holding on to. You have to stop blaming everyone on your list immediately, or the pain will turn to bitterness and destroy you. You don't have to feel tons better; this isn't about feelings, it's about choosing to release them from any debt you might think they owe you. So here we go. This is what you are going to pray for everyone you need to forgive. Even yourself.

Heavenly Father, I am sorry that I have held a grudge against (name of person). Right now I choose to forgive (name the person) from my heart for all the things he/she did to me. I let them go free. They do not owe me anything; they are debt free. I release them to your hands. Now release your love through me. I know I can't do this on my own, so let your forgiveness and love flow through me to him/her. Now, like your Word tells me to, I pray for them to receive your blessings in the name of Jesus. Amen.

Now go back and do that for each person you have been blaming. Get that business cleared up so we can get down to the business of starting over.

Tell it. No, I don't want you to run off and blab it to your buds. Find someone you trust. An adult who you think has a great relationship with God. Sit down with them and tell it. Confess it. James, the brother of Jesus who is the Christ, wrote in his letter (5:16) that we should confess our sins to each other and pray for each other so that we may be healed.

Telling God is about forgiveness. Telling others is about being healed. See, Christ doesn't just want you forgiven, he wants you healed. Complete. So tell it to this person you trust, and let them pray for you. That will get you on the road to total completeness. Your physical virginity is gone, but God wants to restore your emotional and spiritual virginity.

Fill the cup. Your life is a cup. You fill it up with all kinds of stuff. What just happened is, through grace from the Savior, God gave you a do-over. He just emptied all the junk out of your cup, washed it clean, and dried it out. Now your life is going to be whatever you choose to put in your cup.

Some salty suggestions are pray, read the Bible, get hooked up with a church, get Scripture in your head. And the question is *How?* Well, there are bunches of ways to find out about these things. Books, tapes, a youth pastor—keep digging and asking about how to do this stuff. All you have to do is search for it. And, like the truth we have all heard, "Seek and ye shall find."

You had sex. You can't do anything about that.

It's up to you whether you do it again.

Rupert the Fact-Finding Ferret says:

Say you had sex when you were 15, and then you committed to stay pure, and you did. The average age to get married is 25. You've had 10 years of purity. That's 10 years of God healing your spirit and emotions. Hey, you're pure!

Myth #49

• • •

The media
doesn't impact
whether
people
have sex.

A huge reason that teens get into sex is because they are searching for meaning, significance, and belonging. It is a search for God. This isn't me talking some churchy hokey-pokey trying to turn yourself about. Science is proving this stuff.

Check it. A new study just came out that is so fresh it still has that new car smell. It was from Dartmouth Medical School, and it's called *Hardwired to Connect*. Check it out later. It says the spiritual experience is deeply embedded in the human brain.

This makes so much sense. See, God decided to give us free will. We get to choose what we do and how we live. God's ultimate plan is for us to love him and to let him love us. He wants us to connect with him, but he would not force us. He won't jack with our free will to choose. **So what he did was this:** He wired humans with a need to ask, "Why am I here?" "What is the purpose of life?" "What will happen when I die?" "How should I live?" And he made us to ask these questions because he is the answer. He does everything he can to impress, convince, love, and romance people to find the answers in him. But he does not *make* them.

God holds the answers to those questions, but there's a problem with you just walking up and doing a little Q&A with the Almighty. And that is, you can't get to him. In fact, Jesus, the Son of God, said, "No one comes to the Father except through me." Jesus is the only way you can get to God. Therefore, Jesus is the only way to get to the answers to those questions that are deeply woven into your humanity.

I know to some of you this is a bunch of yadda-blah. So let's break it down for the bottom-liners.

Humans are hardwired to search for meaning.

God has the answers to our questions.

The only way to get to God and the answers is through Jesus.

Let's get to the Source. It's time to quit playing and start living life to the fullest. Here's the way it goes: You just pray and ask God to save you. Simple. If you have already done this, rage on. But for those of you who haven't or aren't sure, here's the deal. You're gonna talk to God. He can hear you. Just say something like this:

God, I know that I mess up. I am a sinner. There is no way I can get to you. But I believe that Jesus was your Son, that he died on a cross to pay for all the bad stuff I have done, and that he rose from the dead and beat Satan. I give my life to you right now. It is no longer mine but yours. I want you to be the Guide and the Lord of my life. Thank you for saving me from hell and from my mistakes. And thank you for giving me a new life and a fresh start.

If you just did that, you need to truly understand what just happened. Before, you were an outsider. You could see God or sense that he was around, but you were walking around outside the fence and could not get in. But now, you are a member of the family. Not only do you get to be in the same place with God when you die, but you just got an all-access pass to him. You can talk with him anytime. You are his child. His kid. He will do whatever he can to fulfill your every dream. Why? Because he is going to start shaping the way you dream. If you keep getting to know him more and more, he will pour out his heart to you. You will have an inside look at what he wants you to do, why you are here, and how you should live.

Now, there are some of you who have totally gotten away from God. You are a Christian, but no one could really tell by looking at you and watching the way you act. Now you are really wanting to change, but you don't know where to start. Well, here's how. You do a little God-talk and tell him something like this:

Father, I have turned my back on you. I'm sorry. I want to come back. I confess that I have (fill in the blank with everything you need forgiveness for). Thank you for forgiving me. I give you the control of my life. Give me the strength to let you have it and not take it back. Thank you for loving me and for welcoming me back.

There is a party going on in heaven right now! Remember the story in the Bible about the son who left and blew all his cash and then came back to his dad and asked to work for him as a servant? The dad hugged him and threw a huge party because his kid came home. That is what is happening for you right now.

If you prayed either one of these, here is what I want you to do. First, go tell it. Get a youth pastor, other Christian friends, someone at a church, and tell them what you did. Ask them to help you with it so that you will keep rolling and become what God is designing you to be. Next, go to www.RUdateable.com and let us know what happened. Fill us in so we can get our prayer on for you.

The answers to all your questions can be found in God. He is the reason for your questions and the source for your answers. Stick with him and he will stick with you.

It takes from 2 days

to many years

for an STD

to show symptoms.

Myth #2,354

• • •

This is the coolest book ever.

**(We can't claim coolest ever,
there are a few others
that can compete for that title.
See below for a few others.)**

The *Dirt* is **Done**

You made it. You got through *The Dirt on Sex.* Maybe you got some knowledge. Maybe you got some power. Or maybe you got offended. But you got the truth.

We don't want to just leave you hanging here. If you have Qs or want to chat with someone to get stuff off your chest, come connect with a lot of other people just like you at www.RUdateable.com. We don't know everything, but we can help you figure it out, kick you in the right direction, or just sit and listen.

Understand this: You are important. Believe it! You are loved and loveable. No matter what you have done or not done. How you feel or don't feel. You are valuable, and so is your body. Protect it and you will truly be *Dateable.*

Justin Lookadoo—the name says it all. He's a freak, let's just be frank. But even freaks can have a point, and Justin's is sharp enough to cut your heart out and serve it to you on a platter. He has an amazing ability to take simple truth and make you say, "Duh, why didn't I think of that?" And with this simple truth he'll turn your world upside down.

Justin has been doing this kind of stuff from stages for the past 12 years, yes, since he was just a pup. He was a juvenile probation officer for 5½ years in the toughest part of East Texas. And just a few years ago he left the jail business to tour the U.S., speaking in public schools and at leadership conferences like MADD, DARE, and FFA. He speaks all over the country, so if you want him in your school or church, check out his web site for more info. Hopefully some day you'll get to see the tall one in person and allow him to Lookadoo ya.

In the meantime, check out one of his many books out there. He wrote *Step Off, The Hardest 30 Days of Your Life*. And boy, is it. Don't try this one unless you are prepared to work your butt off in the wildest adventure you've ever had. He also wrote *Extreme Encounters*, a year-long devotional that doesn't scold you as much as *Step Off*. Oh, and yeah, there's also *Ask Hayley/Ask Justin*, a really rockin' book that answers all those freaky questions you might have about dating, love, sex, and the opposite sex. And don't forget about the best-sellers *Dateable* and *The Dateable Rules*.